Dear Parent:
Your child's love of ⟨barcode⟩ re!

Every child learns to read in a di⟨...⟩ ⟨...⟩wn speed.
You can help your young reader ⟨...⟩ ⟨...⟩ome more confident
by encouraging his or her own interests and abilities. You can also guide
your child's spiritual development by reading stories with biblical values
and Bible stories, like I Can Read! books published by Zonderkidz. From
books your child reads with you to the first books he or she reads alone,
there are I Can Read! books for every stage of reading:

SHARED READING
Basic language, word repetition, and whimsical
illustrations, ideal for sharing with your emergent reader.

BEGINNING READING
Short sentences, familiar words, and simple concepts for
children eager to read on their own.

READING WITH HELP
Engaging stories, longer sentences, and language play
for developing readers.

READING ALONE
Complex plots, challenging vocabulary, and high-interest
topics for the independent reader.

ADVANCED READING
Short paragraphs, chapters, and exciting themes for the
perfect bridge to chapter books.

I Can Read! books have introduced children to the joy of reading since
1957. Featuring award-winning authors and illustrators and a fabulous
cast of beloved characters, I Can Read! books set the standard for
beginning readers.

A lifetime of discovery begins with the magical words **"I Can Read!"**

Visit _www.icanread.com_ for information on enriching your child's reading experience.
Visit _www.zonderkidz.com_ for more Zonderkidz I Can Read! titles.

God saw all that he had made,
and it was very good.
—Genesis 1:31

ZONDERKIDZ

God's Great Creation
Copyright © 2014 by Zonderkidz
Illustrations © 2014 by David Miles

Requests for information should be addressed to:

Zonderkidz, 3900 Sparks Drive, Grand Rapids, Michigan 49546

ISBN 978-0-310-73238-9

Art direction and design: Kris Nelson/StoryLook Design

Printed in China

14 15 16 17 18 19 /DSC / 21 20 19 18 17 16 15 14 13 12 11 10 9 8 7 6 5 4 3 2 1

I Can Read!™

ZONDERkidz

READING WITH HELP 2

Adventure BIBLE

God's Great Creation

Pictures by David Miles

ZONDERkidz

God spent six days creating his world.

That first day, God made light.

He said, "Let there be light," and
there it was.

He made sure the light was

separate from the dark.

He called the light "day" and

the dark he called "night."

The second day God

looked at the water and knew

he should separate it.

He made seas and oceans and sky.

On day three, God made dry ground.

He called it land.

Then God said, "Let the land produce plants!"

Every kind of plant was created.

It was all good!

The sun, moon, and stars
were formed on the fourth day.

These lit up the sky and would
help with telling time.

Then, on the fifth day,

God made amazing creatures.

He made creatures that lived in the seas.

He created birds for the skies.

It was all good.

God knew the sixth day was special.

He made man!

Man was God's best creation of all!

Everything was complete!

God blessed the man, Adam, with all

the rest of creation—

man could use it all.

God blessed the man with

a helper too.

This helper's name was Eve.

God put Adam into a deep sleep.

He took one of Adam's ribs

and created her.

Then God said to Adam and Eve, "Use all you see with respect. And follow my one rule: do not eat from the tree of knowledge of good and evil."

God was happy.

Adam and Eve were happy.

The garden and all in it

was very good.

And so God rested

on the seventh day.

Adam and Eve lived happily
in the garden. Then one day
Satan had a plan.

He went to the woman as a snake and said,
"Did God really say you must not eat
from any tree in the garden?"

Eve said, "No. God said we can eat
from any tree. But not the one
in the middle of the garden."
"Nothing bad will happen to you,
Eve. You will be like God!
You will know all about good
and evil," the snake said.

Eve liked that idea.

So Eve took a bite of the fruit.

Then she offered it to Adam.

He took a bite too.

Awhile later God called to Adam and Eve.

God said, "Where are you?"

Adam answered, "Eve and I are here.

But we are afraid and hid."

God asked, "Why are you afraid?

Did you eat from the tree

I told you not to eat from?"

Adam said, "Yes,

the woman gave it to me."

Eve said, "The snake fooled me.

I ate it too." God was very sad.

He said to the snake, "I must punish you.

Humans will not like you.

You will crawl on your belly

and eat dust."

God punished Adam and Eve too.
He said, "You cannot live in
the garden anymore."
Adam and Eve left the garden.
Angels were sent to take care
of the garden now.

But God did not stop loving

Adam and Eve.

As they left the garden, God was

planning how to help

his people.

People in Bible Times

"God created mankind in his own image,
in the image of God
he created them."
GENESIS 1:27

Adam

God created man in his likeness.
God made Adam from the dust
of the ground, and he breathed
life into him. Adam had lots of
responsibilities in the Garden of
Eden. He even got to name
the animals!

Eve

God did not want Adam to be
all alone and so he created Eve,
using one of Adam's ribs. Eve
was meant to live with Adam
and share his responsibilities
in the Garden.

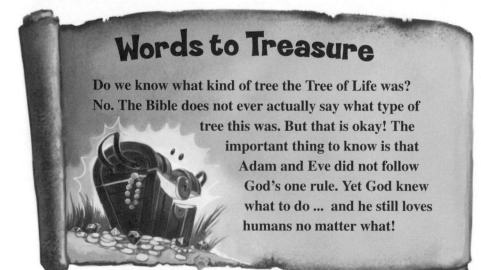

Words to Treasure

Do we know what kind of tree the Tree of Life was?
No. The Bible does not ever actually say what type of
tree this was. But that is okay! The
important thing to know is that
Adam and Eve did not follow
God's one rule. Yet God knew
what to do ... and he still loves
humans no matter what!